Shadow

Michael Sherlock

BookLeaf Publishing

India | USA | UK

Presentation by *BookLeaf Publishing*

Web: www.bookleafpub.com

E-mail: info@bookleafpub.com

ISBN: 9789358317039

First edition 2023

Love

When is there a time, where you are not lurking
in the dark
An unexpected candlelight, an unexpected spark
You light the days of man, and set the world
aglow
A feeling of a quiet peace, that everyone should
know

I have felt you more than once, breathing in my
chest
An inner warmth and smile, calming me at rest
I have seen you in a child's eyes, shining bright
as gold
And even in a dying breath, for the ones of old

But now I wonder where you are, a mystery to
me
You are hiding in the world somewhere, and
very hard to see
My body is almost empty now, a quiet meager
shell
Almost empty and need some love, as far as I
can tell

Tired

Tired as I am through the day
Hope is just a stranger
I wait for calm
How long must I wait?

You have many others under your grip
Looking for their own solitude
Wanting for a light
How long must they wait?

We just wait longer
We just wait heavier
Filled with sadness
How long must we wait?

But who made the rules on happiness?
Who made the rules on hope?
I see you getting closer now
I...will not wait

Mind

Mind born quiet; into the busy light.
A busy mind grown tired; fading into night.

What happens in between is for us to figure out
Makes no sense at all, with faith or without

How many lives must we live until we learn it
all
How many lives must we waste until the last
ones fall

We scream and cry, point and shout over what
other people do
But your troubled mind and body only lead to
you

So take your tears and worries and let them float
away
That moment is not forever, that moment is just
today

We have tomorrow to make a difference,
something bright and new
Let memories be memories, not tarnishing your
view

So rise above the past, may the future me discussed
Today is all that matters, that day depends on us

Among the Trees

We don't listen to the trees today
Too distracted by our lives

Just scrolling, clicking, searching
Until dopamine arrives

We distract ourselves with every thought
As if our lives depend

But thumb speed matters not at all
When real life comes to end

My views on policy matter not
And influencing not my game

But is it that important to you
How many people know your name

Hats off to you if you have success
And have spread your wealth and joy

But nothing comes with you in the end
Not even the smallest toy

The Monster

One day appeared a monster
Created from the absence of love

A monster with a heart of gold
A gift from light above

But now that heart is tarnished
Aged by you and me

A heart that no longer shines
No longer for all to see

What will polish this monsters heart
And why is this heart so old

The monster needs to step into the light
This monster needs to come out of the cold

For underneath this monster is good
Underneath this monster is hope

So monster turn your face to the sun
Come off from the end of that rope

So the monster turned his face to the light

And climbed as fast as he can

And low and behold the surprise
The monster was just a man

Time

You rule as if a king, with ruthless force and might
And with us everyday, whether day and night
Easier on the young, but observant to the old
But all so eager, to see your story unfold

We see you in the mirror, much to our dismay
You gather many taxes, and all of us must pay
You have grown rich in your collection, a universal box of wealth
No fear of your collections safety, not one is of the stealth

I pray someday we take your thrown, and beat you at your game
At first we will laugh at you, and gather power and fame
But then again you are the king, and no one can compete
So now we bow and praise, and tremble at your feet

The Past

I see you when I fall asleep
You come to me in dreams

And if they're dreams of darker times
I can almost hear the screams

You follow me from place to place
Without any permission from me

And cloud my judgement everyday
Sometimes reality is hard to see

You've conditioned my mind and my heart
Why can't you leave me alone?

Because today I want to live in today
And your rule will be overthrown

The Sun

Do you know what you give?
Another chance of life for another day

You are different to everyone
Another chance for children to play

You bring warmth to the world
And don't expect anything back

You can make someone's day
But when you're missing it's black

I love to see you in the morning
Emitting such energy and strength

But yet I feel sad
When I don't see you at length

I just want to thank you
And I know you don't care

You are our protector
And existence is rare

Heart

You've been with me from the beginning
A dance within my chest

Not sure who's in control
So lonely in your nest

I've felt you in the good times
But so painful in the bad

I've felt you when I sleep
So heavy when I'm sad

How long will you let me stay here
A thought for everyday

Can I please stay a while?
There's still so much I have to say

I hope I can fill you with hope
I can show you love and joy

Please keep me here forever
Because I am just a boy

Disguise

We all wear other faces
A different face for a different day
A face for times of struggle
And a face for times of play

What do these faces mean?
Is there a story to be told,
These faces have been made in vein,
All of them get old.

You all put on your faces,
In the morning and the night
You hide your pain and struggle
That doesn't make it right

Do you have a real face?
A face kissed by wind and sun?
That's the face I want to see,
The face when your heart begun

Show that face to everyone,
And let it shine like polished gold.
This face was made just for you,
All of them get old.

Alcohol

You emptied my emotions and brought me to my
knees
But yet not that long ago, you put my mind at
ease

I though that we were friends and you convinced
me that were true
A friend that would keep me warm, the best
friend I ever knew

But now this friendship has turned its ugly face
And brought me to a tougher time, a dark and
lonely place

Now we must part our ties and go our separate
ways
You will no longer be part of my sadness, or all
of life's delays

There's life out there, a life of love and hope
And not a dying soul at the end of an iron rope

I choose to go the other way, I choose to find the
light

I choose to throw in the towel, I choose to lose
the fight

So it's goodbye forever, there's never coming
back
You can not take my happiness, that's something
I will not lack

Tomorrow

A futile battle, yesterdays problems
An anxiety riddled mind
Trying to change the landscape
Of what is forever

Prior lapses of judgment
So small at the time
Suffocate your mind
Today is cloaked in mystery

Undo the woven noise
The yarns made of a noisy past
Let go let go let go
They lie about the now

We all get a canvas
A block of granite
But most of us use a brush on a granite
And a chisel on the canvas

So take tomorrow as it comes
And take your medium each new day
Create a masterpiece worthy of note
Your heart is all you need

Sunset

I have forgotten the way you present yourself
Only once in a while do I notice how unique you
are
An ode to the day past, a reminder to myself
Yet the beauty painted from something afar

Never once the same from one spot
A miracle of the universe everyday
Something noticed by all you are not
A visual anomaly made different by each ray

Perseverance

The wind presses against you
Like all the stars you can see
You stare out into the ocean
And spot a small bird
Just trying to stay afloat
The bird has no where to go
And does not know when the wind will cease
The bird just has to point its head
Into the wind
If the bird turns it will get slapped
Down into the ocean and drown
It has no choice but to keep going
Straight into the wind
The bird does not know
When the wind will stop

Life

A grasp of frozen dirt with drops of forgotten
tears
Is all it comes down to, no matter how many
years

Winters many and old friends passed
How long will this puppet last

There has been hard days, but mostly good
And oh so loved the passed days I've stood

We fall in love, maybe once or twice
And if you're lucky, hit with rice

When you're young, life's a dream
A family, your friends, your heart, your team

You come into this world, free body and mind
May you never forget, you're one of a kind

As Is

We close our eyes and feel our way through the
dark
Only briefly do we open them to check in the
direction that we sail

Time and time again we drown out the voice of
reason and truth
And are bewildered that we find ourselves off
rail

When young we discover by accident and
question everything in sight
We turn over every stone and reach out beyond
our mind

Through unfavorable experience, our discovery
fades away
And our eyes begin to shut as the world becomes
unkind

How do we save these souls that let their eyes
shut forever.
Let them only close their eyes seconds
longer than a blink

Save them from the lie they tell themselves
A helping hand is more powerful than you think

Shadow

A shadow behind me, a weight
You are all I see in the mirror
Everywhere I see you
Don't you sleep or rest?

You are in every room hiding
Forever, lurking
Taking over my soul
Why don't you sleep?

I am growing stronger now
I no longer need you
The lessons have been taught
Can't you see?

So farewell now enemy
Can't you just go?
I am tired
Why don't you sleep.

Struggle

We find ourselves in a struggle at times
An obstacle big or small
We find ourselves in moral dilemmas
A time that questions our souls

But how to we respond to these tests
These tests of integrity and valor
A different response of course
For each of us throughout time

We must respect the opinion of all
Unless in the harm of other man
We must observe all the answers
Unless in the harm of freedom

But yet we do nothing of the sort
We persecute opinion
And we persecute the truth
And we steal freedom from the all

Rush

Time is treated poorly
By most humans on this rock

We push off till tomorrow
The ones in rush we all mock

Or do they see something different
A different hourglass in mind

And just simply value seconds
While we move forward blind

Mock not what you don't see
They see the truth within the day

As one thing's guaranteed
No one gets to stay

Moment

Let my words be the path to my dreams
And let those embers burn as bright as the sun

Words have delivered men to the throne
And words have displaced kings to the worms

Lost in translation has taken on a new meaning
An avoidable penalty since time has begun

Words have lost their value
So who decides the terms?